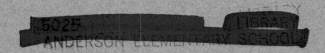

KANSAS CITY
CHIEFS

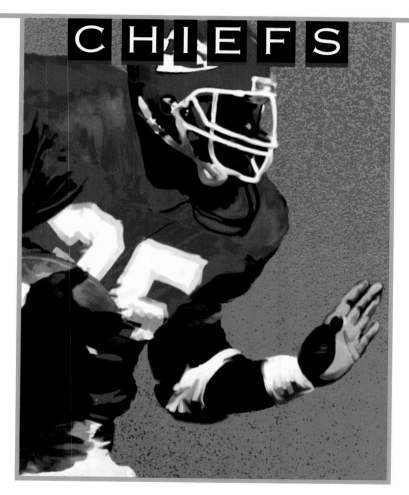

RICHARD RAMBECK

CREATIVE ● EDUCATION INC.

Published by Creative Education, Inc.
123 S. Broad Street, Mankato, Minnesota 56001

Designed by Rita Marshall

Cover illustration by Lance Hidy Associates

Photos by Allsport USA, Bettmann Archives, Duomo, Spectra-
Action and Sportschrome

Library of Congress Cataloging-in-Publication Data

Rambeck, Richard.
   Kansas City Chiefs/Richard Rambeck.
   p. cm.
   ISBN 0-88682-370-6
   1. Kansas City Chiefs (Football team)—History. I. Title.
GV956.K35R36 1990
796.332′64′09778411—dc20   90-41076
                                 CIP

Kansas City is the second-largest city in the state of Missouri. Kansas City is also the second-largest city in the state of Kansas. Confused? It's simple, although sometimes it doesn't seem that way. There are two Kansas Cities, and they are right next to each other. The Kansas City in Missouri is located at the western edge of the state. The Kansas City in Kansas is at the eastern edge of that state. If you drive westward out of Kansas City, Missouri, you don't have far to go to get to Kansas City, Kansas.

There are two Kansas Cities, both of them located on the Missouri River. But this is the story of only one of them —the one in Missouri. It is a city of almost 450,000 citizens,

All-time Kansas City great Len Dawson.

which makes it almost three times as big as the other Kansas City. Kansas City, Missouri, is also home to the only pro football team based in either Missouri or Kansas—the Kansas City Chiefs.

1 9 6 0

Cowboys or Indians? The Chiefs were originally known as the Dallas Texans.

The Chiefs didn't start out in Kansas City, though. The team began play in 1960 and was known as the Dallas Texans. When the American Football League was formed in 1960, the Texans were one of the original eight teams. Their owner, Lamar Hunt, was a Texan, and he wanted his team to play in his home state. But Hunt had a problem. The Texans weren't the only pro football team in Dallas. The same year the AFL began play, the older, more established National Football League put an expansion team in Dallas known as the Cowboys. The NFL wasn't about to let the AFL have Dallas without a fight. As it turned out, it would be a losing battle for Hunt and the AFL.

The Dallas fans never really fell in love with the Texans. The Cowboys had bigger crowds even though they lost almost every game in 1960 and 1961. The Texans were losing money, and Hunt knew something had to be done. The franchise could either fold or move to another city. "There is no decision to be made," Hunt said. "This team means too much to me. It will never fold, not as long as I'm the owner."

DAWSON PASSES THE TEST IN THE AFL

While Hunt looked for another city to move his team to, the Texans and their coach, Hank Stram, prepared to play the 1962 season. In training camp that year was a new quarterback who had played five years in the NFL. Lenny Dawson had been with the Pittsburgh Steelers

In the '80s Bill Kenney struggled to replace Dawson.

TD Man! The club record for the most touchdowns in a season, nineteen, was set by running back Abner Hayes.

and the Cleveland Browns, and he was considered a good player with a lot of potential. But both Cleveland and Pittsburgh decided to let him go. They would regret that decision.

Stram watched Dawson closely during training camp. The coach knew that Dawson was probably the best quarterback he had. Stram had been an assistant at Purdue University when Dawson played there. But Stram had noticed something about Dawson that concerned him. Dawson wasn't the same quarterback Stram had seen at Purdue and in the NFL. He wasn't as good as Stram thought he'd be. One day, Stram went over to talk to his new quarterback.

"I'm going to be very frank with you and tell you I'm surprised to detect some of the things you're doing out there," Stram told Dawson. "I never realized how many bad habits you've developed. You have your work cut out for you. I know you can do the job, but we'll have to reach back and put it all together again."

Dawson was shocked. He figured he would have no problem becoming the Chiefs' quarterback. Stram had given him a wake-up call. Now it was Dawson's job to rise to the occasion. Later that day, Dawson spoke to Stram. "Believe me, Hank, I had no idea that I've gotten so out of the groove," Dawson said. "The trouble is, nobody ever worked with me or talked to me about technique or execution during the five years I spent in the NFL. However, I'm ready to buckle down and work under your direction."

Stram was impressed with Dawson's reaction. The coach had sent his message, and it had been received. Led by Dawson the Texans rolled to an 11-3 record and won the Western Division of the AFL. Helping Dawson and

Stram were halfback Abner Haynes, who scored twenty-one touchdowns to set a league record, and fullback Curtis McClinton, who was named AFL Rookie of the Year. The defense was also strong, led by linemen Buck Buchanon and Jerry Mays, and linebackers E.J. Holub and Bobby Bell.

In the 1962 league championship game, Dallas beat its Texas rivals, the Houston Oilers, 20-17 in sudden-death overtime. Dawson was named AFL Player of the Year. Yet despite the success, the Dallas fans did not support the team. Attendance at games was disappointing. As a result, after the season, the Texans moved to Kansas City and became the Chiefs.

The change of scenery also changed the team's luck. The Texans had finished as winners. The Chiefs didn't start out that way. Kansas City wound up third in the Western Division in 1963 with a 5-7-2 record. But the team, with Dawson becoming perhaps the best quarterback in the AFL, battled back.

Pass attack? The Chiefs racked up a grand total of zero rushing yards against Denver on December 19!

CHIEFS RECEIVE A GIFT IN OTIS TAYLOR

The Chiefs improved, but they still hadn't returned to championship status. They needed more weapons; in 1965 the Chiefs found one. They drafted a wide receiver with a world of talent. Kansas City scout Lloyd Wills couldn't believe how good Otis Taylor was. "I thought when I first saw him and still think now that for pure natural ability, there has never been anyone like Otis," Wills commented. "He can do what he wants to do. When I go out now and look at wide receivers, I compare them to Otis."

What made Taylor special was his size and strength. He

The Chiefs stretched for greatness in the 1960s, (pages 10–11).

9

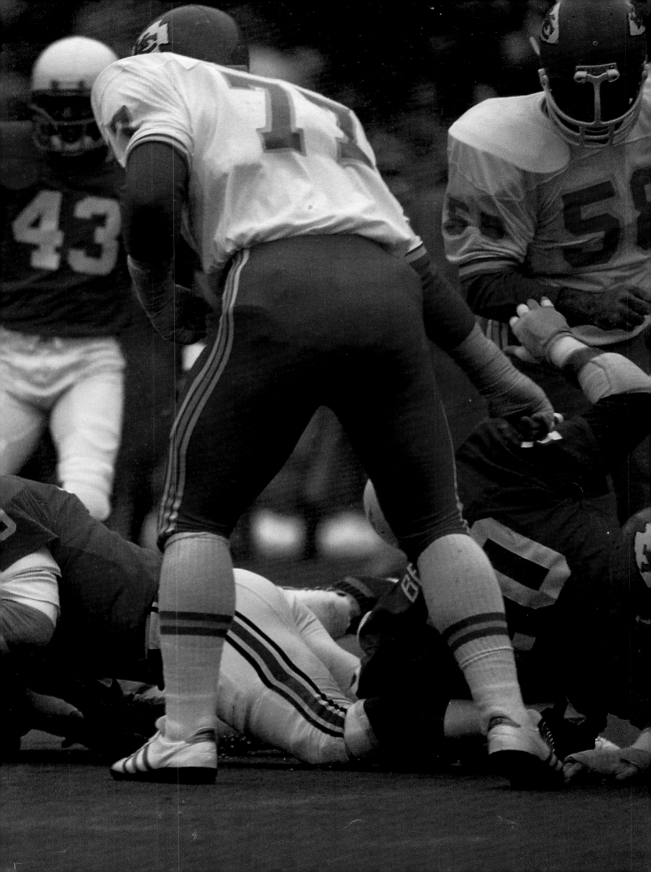

Kansas City wide receiver Otis Taylor led the team with fifty-eight pass receptions.

was huge by wide receiver standards, six feet three and 215 pounds. Some linebackers weren't even that big. "Some receivers have great speed and great moves," Dawson said. "Otis has both plus size and strength. He has a great deal of confidence and recognizes what defenses are trying to do against him. He's a complete player."

Taylor knew exactly how good he was. He demanded a lot from himself and was never satisfied with anything less than excellence. "I'll tell you something about Otis Taylor," Taylor said. "He wants to be the best—always. There hasn't been a year when he didn't want to score more touchdowns than anybody and gain more yardage than anybody. At the start of the season, I aim for the top ten and higher. And I don't quit."

The Chiefs didn't quit in 1966 until they had won the Western Division and then defeated the Buffalo Bills in the league championship game. In past years the season ended after the AFL title game. Not in 1966. The AFL champion Chiefs played the NFL champs, the Green Bay Packers. The game was called the AFL-NFL Championship Game. Lamar Hunt didn't like that name. He thought it was too long, and too clumsy to say. "Why don't we just call it the Super Bowl," Hunt suggested. So that's what everybody called a game that was officially known as the AFL-NFL Championship Game. Super Bowl, though, would stick as a name. Credit Lamar Hunt for that.

The Chiefs weren't given much of a chance to defeat the powerful Packers. After all, the experts said, everybody knew the NFL was a much better league. In fact, many considered the AFL to be a minor league compared with the NFL. But the fans were obviously curious to see how the game would come out. More than 65 million people watched the game on television, the largest single audience for an athletic event in the history of television.

What the viewers saw was the Chiefs matching Green Bay's early score with one of their own, tying the game 7-7 in the second quarter on Dawson's seven-yard pass to fullback Curtis McClinton. Kansas City only trailed 14-10 at halftime, but the Chiefs ran out of gas in the second half. Behind quarterback Bart Starr, the Packers ran away to a 35-10 victory. Green Bay managed to shut down Kansas City's offense in the second half, bottling up Otis Taylor and running back Mike Garrett, as well as putting pressure on Dawson every time he tried to throw.

Uff-da! The Chiefs acquired Norwegian Jan Stenerud, who had come to the U.S. on a skiing scholarship.

All the experts had expected the Chiefs to lose. After all, they said, the older NFL was clearly a better league than the AFL. Those experts would soon be singing a different tune. In 1968 the New York Jets shocked the football world. The Jets, champs of the AFL, defeated NFL champion Baltimore 16-7 in Super Bowl III. The experts weren't impressed. A fluke, they called it. Wait till next year, they said. Next year was 1969, and the AFL champ was Kansas City.

The Chiefs had taken a weird route to the title. They finished second in the Western Division, but then won playoff games over the New York Jets and the Oakland Raiders, which allowed Kansas City to become the first AFL team to play in two Super Bowls. The opponent this time was the Minnesota Vikings. The odds makers said the Vikings were thirteen-point favorites, but the Chiefs weren't impressed. This was a different Kansas City team than the one that lost in Super Bowl I. Dawson sensed that right

Accuracy! The Chiefs finished an NFL record four seasons leading the league in pass completions.

after the Chiefs beat Oakland in the AFL title game. "I got a great indication of the feeling of the players when one of my linemen came up to me and said, 'Don't worry about it. We can beat these guys,'" Dawson said.

A newspaper reporter asked Dawson if the Chiefs were going to have a problem with Carl Eller, Minnesota's All-Pro defensive end. Before Dawson could answer the question, David Hill, the Kansas City lineman who would have to block Eller, came over and put his hand on Dawson's shoulder. "Eller isn't going to touch you," Hill shouted. "Don't worry about it. He had better bring his lunch, because he's going to have to fight me all the way down the line."

"We were ready for the Vikings," Dawson reflected. But he had other worries. A couple of days before the Super Bowl, a report surfaced that linked Dawson to professional gamblers. The Kansas City quarterback was accused of betting on pro football games, including those played by the Chiefs. If true, such charges could lead to a lifetime ban from football. But these charges had nothing to back them up. The rumors bothered Dawson. They angered his teammates as well. The Chiefs were now even more ready than before.

Kansas City dominated the Vikings in the first half. Dawson directed the team on three long drives, but the Chiefs couldn't get the ball in the end zone. They had to settle for three Jan Stenerud field goals. Late in the half, Dawson drove Kansas City to the Viking five yard line. On third down Minnesota's defenders braced for an expected pass. Dawson rolled out to his right, but then handed the ball to

Current Kansas City star Christian Okoye.

Mike Garrett, who ran back to the left and into the end zone. The Vikings were stunned. They also were behind 16-0.

In the second half, the Vikings scored a touchdown early in the third quarter. It appeared the momentum had swung Minnesota's way. But Dawson and the Chiefs responded to the challenge. From the Viking forty-six, Dawson faded back and threw a sideline pass to Taylor. Although it was a play designed to get a first down and not much more, Taylor had other ideas. "It was only a six-yard pass," he said. "I got hit on the left side and spun out. Then I hit the last guy downfield with my hand. I always try to punish a pass defender, just as he does me. I wanted to score that touchdown."

Taylor, who broke two hard tackles before scoring, gave the Chiefs a 23-7 lead on the remarkable forty-six yard pass and run. Dawson knew the game was over. "That was the touchdown I wanted," Dawson said. "I knew we had them. . . . I could sense the frustrations of the Minnesota defense. They weren't able to do the things they had been doing all year against the NFL teams."

The game ended 23-7. The scoreboard in Tulane Stadium in New Orleans said Super Chiefs in huge letters. And they had been super. They destroyed a team that was supposed to win by two touchdowns. Dawson, who was named Player of Game, had an almost flawless contest, completing twelve of seventeen passes. In the locker room afterward, reporters asked Dawson how the Chiefs had been able to move the ball consistently against the best defense in football. "Our game plan really wasn't very

1 9 7 0

Len Dawson and Robert Holmes were key factors during the Chiefs drive to the Super Bowl.

16

complicated," Dawson said. "It involved throwing a lot of formations at them—formations they hadn't seen during the course of the season."

The Chiefs had risen to the top of the NFL, and they had every reason to believe they would stay on top. Their offense had the accuracy and efficiency of Dawson, the strength and speed of Taylor, and the quickness and toughness of Mike Garrett. On defense the stars were defensive end Buck Buchanan, middle linebacker Willie Lanier, outside linebacker Bobby Bell, and safety Johnny Robinson.

When the NFL and AFL merged in 1970, the Chiefs were placed in the American Football Conference Western Division along with the Oakland Raiders, Denver Broncos, and San Diego Chargers. It was a strong division because both the Chiefs and Raiders had powerful teams. Oakland won the AFC West in 1970, but Kansas City took the division title in 1971. That earned the Chiefs the right to host the Miami Dolphins in the first round of the playoffs. The game was on Christmas Day, but for a while it appeared a winner wouldn't be decided until after the New Year.

Dawson hit Elmo Wright on a sixty-three yard touchdown pass to give the Chiefs a 24-17 lead in the fourth quarter. Miami tied the score with ninety seconds left. Dawson then drove Kansas City into field-goal range, but the usually reliable Jan Stenerud missed the kick. The game went into sudden-death overtime, but there would not be anything sudden about the ending to this game.

Both Stenerud and Dolphins' kicker Garo Yepremian had chances to kick the game winner in the fifth quarter,

1 9 7 1

All for nothing— The Chiefs played the longest game in NFL history only to lose to Miami.

The explosive Chief offensive, (pages 18–19).

Stolen! Super thief Emmett Thomas intercepted twelve passes during the season.

but both missed. The game went into the sixth period. It was only the second time in pro football history that a sixth quarter was needed. Ironically, the only other time was 1962, when the Dallas Texans, later to become the Chiefs, defeated the Houston Oilers in the AFL championship game. This time the Chiefs would wind up losers. Yepremian got another chance midway through the sixth quarter. His field goal split the uprights, and the Dolphins won 27-24. The longest game in NFL history was finally over. To this day no NFL game has lasted any longer than the eighty-two minutes and forty seconds the Chiefs and Dolphins battled.

The game was the last ever played in Kansas City's Municipal Stadium. Unfortunately for the Chiefs, the game was also the last postseason game the team would play for fifteen years. The Chiefs moved to the new Arrowhead Stadium in 1972. It was a gorgeous place to play, with almost eighty thousand seats, thirty thousand more than Municipal Stadium had. While the Chiefs kept winning in 1972 and 1973, they didn't make the playoffs. After a 5-9 season in 1974, Stram was fired. A year later both Dawson and Taylor retired. Of Kansas City's championship pieces, only Willie Lanier was left, and he wasn't enough. The team slid to the bottom of the AFC West in the late 1970s and stayed there. The Chiefs just couldn't find a quarterback as effective as Dawson or a running back as good as Mike Garrett. Several backs showed flashes of brilliance—MacArthur Lane, Tony Reed, Ted McKnight—but none could maintain consistent excellence.

DELANEY MAKES BIG, BUT TRAGIC, IMPAPCT

The Chiefs struggled until 1980, when new coach Marv Levy brought the team back to respectability. Kansas City finished 8-8 and expected bigger things in 1981. The addition of a rookie running back in 1981 made Kansas City one of the most improved teams in the NFL. Joe Delaney came out of Northwestern State University in Louisiana. The school was small, and so was Joe, but he was incredibly fast. In his rookie year, Delaney gained 1,121 yards, a Kansas City team record. Not even the great Mike Garrett had rushed for that many yards in a season. In recognition of his efforts, Delaney was named AFC Rookie of the Year.

Behind Delaney the Chiefs nearly made the playoffs in 1981, but late-season injuries and inconsistency at quarterback doomed the team's hopes. Kansas City finished 9-7. The following year a players' strike wiped out almost half the season. Still, Delaney had another solid season. Only a second-year player, Delaney was considered by many experts to be one of the best backs in the game. But on June 29, 1983, on a hot day in Monroe, Louisiana, all that changed—tragically.

Joe Delaney tried to do that day what he tried to do every day—help people. This time it was three young boys swimming in a lake. Delaney was on the shore of the lake playing catch with some friends. Suddenly, he heard cries for help. A little boy ran up to Delaney and said, "Can you swim?"

1 9 8 0

Wide receiver Carlos Carson was drafted by the Chiefs following a successful career at Louisiana State University.

Running back Paul Palmer.

"I can't swim good, but I've got to save those kids," Delaney said. "If I don't come up, get somebody." So Delaney, who wasn't much of a swimmer, jumped in the lake to try to save those three boys.

"He was scared of water any deeper than his waist," said Delaney's sister Lucille. "It was amazing that he would rush in after those boys." But Delaney did rush in, and he didn't come back. One of the boys managed to make it to shore. Two of the boys drowned. Joe Delaney didn't survive either. One of pro football's brightest young stars was dead at age twenty-four.

"People ask me, 'How could Joe have gone in the water the way he did?' " said Delaney's college coach, A. L. Williams. "And I answer, 'Why, he never gave it a second thought, because helping people was a conditioned reflex to Joe Delaney.' "

On July 4, 1983, they had a funeral for Joe Delaney. All of his high school and college friends, teammates and coaches were there. So were Marv Levy and Chiefs' owner Lamar Hunt. Levy got up to speak. "Joe was a person who was genuine and honest right to the core of his being," Levy said.

Then Williams spoke about Delaney. "The first year Joe was up in Kansas City, Les Miller, the Chiefs' director of player personnel, called me on the phone and said, 'I want to talk to you about one of your players.' I thought something was wrong. But then he said, 'I just wanted to tell you that Joe Delaney is the finest young man and the hardest worker we've ever had here.' The sky was the limit for him. We never got to see what Joe Delaney would be."

Joe Delaney was gone, and so were the team's winning ways. In 1983 the Chiefs slipped to last place in the AFC

1 9 8 3

Quarterback Bill Kenney passed for 24 touchdowns and over 4300 yards during the season.

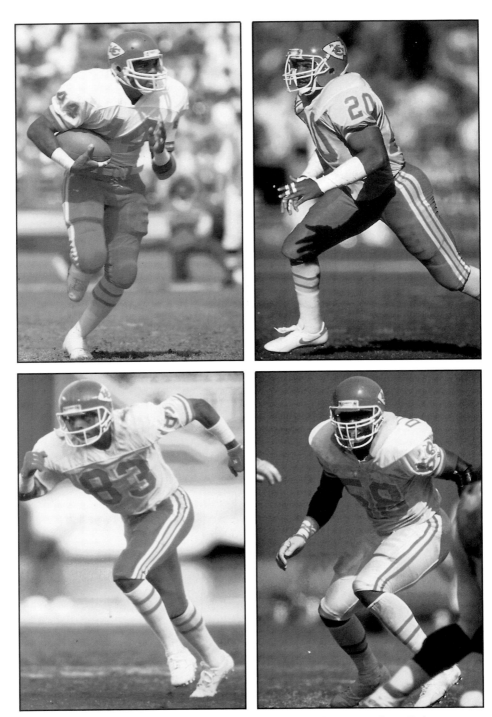

Clockwise: Herman Heard, Deron Cherry, Derrick Thomas, Stephone Paige.

West. Levy was fired and replaced by John Mackovic, who built a winning team thanks to quarterback Bill Kenney and an excellent defense that featured perhaps the finest secondary in the NFL. Safeties Deron Cherry and Lloyd Burruss and cornerbacks Albert Lewis and Kevin Ross made life miserable for opposing quarterbacks. Lewis and Ross were both excellent in one-on-one coverage, while Cherry usually was near the top of the league in interceptions. On offense Kenney had plenty of fine targets to pass to—veterans Henry Marshall and J.T. Smith and young receivers Carlos Carson and Stephone Paige.

Take-away: Safety Deron Cherry led the AFC with nine interceptions during the season.

The improved Chiefs made the playoffs in 1986, losing in the first round to the New York Jets. Despite the success, Mackovic was fired. The players couldn't relate to him, Lamar Hunt said. Frank Ganz replaced Mackovic, but the Chiefs slumped again.

OKOYE IS A BIG HIT IN KANSAS CITY

In Ganz's first year, the Chiefs found a gem in the 1987 draft, a six feet three 260-pound bruiser of a runner named Christian Okoye. Okoye grew up in Nigeria and came to the United States on a track scholarship to Azusa Pacific University in California. When he got to Azusa, Okoye noticed a strange new game called football. He had never played, but this sport seemed like fun. So he asked Azusa's track coach, Dr. Terry Franson, if he could play for Azusa's football team. Franson didn't like the idea. He tried to talk Okoye out of playing football. "Why do you want to play?" Franson asked.

"Because," Okoye said, "I think I could be a professional player." A couple of years later, he was. The Chiefs

Hall of Fame kicker Jan Stenerud, (pages 26–27).

25

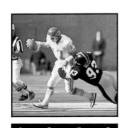

Trusty arm! Veteran quarterback Steve DeBerg had the best pass completion rate in the AFC.

had themselves a Nigerian fullback whom Franson called "one of the best big athletes in the world." Okoye wasn't used that much during Ganz's two years with the Chiefs. But in 1989 new coach Marty Schottenheimer decided the Chiefs had to give Okoye the ball more—a lot more. And Okoye responded by leading the NFL in rushing.

"I can remember Marty asking me, 'How many times do you think you can carry the ball in a game?'" Okoye reflected. "I told him I once carried forty times in college. I told him I often carried thirty times a game at Azusa. Marty was surprised I told him I could do that. It is no problem for me."

Okoye impressed his offensive linemen as well as Schottenheimer. "To feel the force he runs with is amazing," said tackle Irv Eatman. "He has slammed into my back on running plays a few times, and the only way I can describe what it feels like is to imagine standing on the street and getting hit by a car going fifty miles an hour. And he's just getting a head of steam by the time he gets to me. Imagine what it's like to tackle him."

Mike Webster, the Chiefs' center and a seventeen-year veteran, said Okoye may already be one of the best backs ever. "You try to think of who he reminds you of," Webster said. "Earl Campbell is the only guy who comes to mind. But he was thirty-five pounds lighter than Christian, and Christian is probably faster. Look at how Christian is built. The guy ought to be blocking for me."

Carl Peterson, president and general manager of the team, may have summed up the Chiefs' feelings about having Okoye when he said, "It's almost like every day you're opening a Christmas present, because you see something new and so exciting."

The powerful Christian Okoye.

Defensive end Art Still.

All-Pro linebacker Derrick Thomas.

31

1 9 9 0

*More than okay:
Explosive running
back Christian
Okoye bewildered
his opponents with
his powerful
running.*

The Chiefs made rapid improvement in 1989. Okoye and the offense got better and better as the season went along. The defense, led by AFC Defensive Rookie of the Year Derrick Thomas, became one of the best in the league. The defensive backfield still was solid, thanks to Deron Cherry, Lloyd Burruss, and Albert Lewis. Linebacker Dino Hackett combined with nose tackle Bill Maas to make the Chiefs solid against the run.

Offensively, the Chiefs still need to develop a passing attack to complement Okoye's running. Veteran quarterback Steven DeBerg was the starter in 1989, but Steve Pelluer may represent the future for Kansas City. Pelluer, who spent his early years in the NFL with the Dallas Cowboys, has shown potential, but he needs to be more consistent for the Chiefs to become a Super Bowl contender.

The coach, Schottenheimer, is used to winning. He led the Cleveland Browns to three straight AFC Central Division titles before coming to Kansas City. Now with Okoye and a strong defense as a foundation, the Chiefs are ready to recapture the winning ways the team had in the late 1960s and early 1970s. Kansas City fans have not seen a home playoff game since the memorable overtime encounter with Miami in 1971. That may change soon.

Las trece en Punto

Para M.L.S.

Título original: Thirteen O'Clock, 2005

© de la edición original en inglés: Chronicle Books LLC, 2005, en San Francisco, California

© del texto y de las ilustraciones: James Stimson, 2007

© de la traducción: Silvia Pérez Tato, 2007

© de la adaptación: Xosé Ballesteros, 2007

© de esta edición: Faktoría K de libros, 2007
Urzaiz, 125 bajo - 36205 Vigo
Telf.: 986 127 334
faktoria@faktoriakdelibros.com
www.faktoriakdelibros.com

Primera edición: agosto, 2007
Impreso en C/A Gráfica, Vigo

ISBN: 978-84-935804-7-6
DL: PO 457-2007

James Stimson

Las trece en Punto

FAKTORIA K DE LIBROS

E ra alrededor de la medianoche;
las doce cincuenta y nueve, para ser exactos.
El viento soplaba con fuerza
y la vieja casa crujía y crujía.

La niña miraba por la ventana. Era una noche tranquila y normal.
Pero *algo* aguardaba en la casa, en aquella casa tan especial...

En el viejo caserón había un reloj, con números que no contaban hasta doce...

... contaban hasta un escalofriante número **trece.**

13

12 · 1
11 · · 2
10 · · 3
9 · · 4
8 · · 5
7 · 6

Tic Tac,
Tac tic,
Tic tac tic ...

GONG

Sobre el viejo reloj se abrió, de repente,
un oculto ventanuco.
Y cuando sonó la 1ª campanada de las trece en punto,
por él se asomó un duende ESPERPÉNTICO
que estaría mucho mejor
con su nombre grabado en una lápida
y no **tacone**ando en la oscuridad.

Toc, Toc, Toc,
baila un Tictac y un Rock.

¡Ya suena la 2ª campanada!
Con su esquelética llave,
el esqueleto abrió una *pequeña* puerta
y liberó a su **monstruosa** amiga...

La Cosa

Puede que Cosa sea un nombre *raro*,
pero no lo es si la cosa se explica.
Porque una cosa, por sí misma, podría ser cualquier cosa,
pero siempre será una cosa, ¡aunque sea horrorosa!

¿Pero qué es eso? ¿Eso qué es? ¿Qué es lo que da cuerda al reloj?
¿Qué hay ahí dentro que viene y va?
¿Es un curioso péndulo girando sobre un pivote??
¿O quizás es un metrónomo que ha perdido su compás???

¡NO! La vieja maquinaria se dio impulso
para que su *tictac* fuese aún más desquiciante,
y al sonar las campanadas 3ª y 4ª,
el mecanismo se balanceó, saltó, y huyó hacia adelante.

Qué **DeseNtonados** y qué **disONANteS**

tocaron los tres tañidos siguientes hacia las trece en punto...

Mientras tanto...

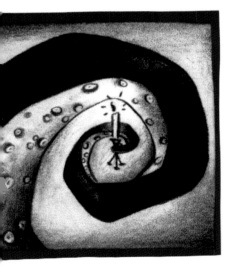

algo viscoso,

algo arácnido,

y *algo* volador,

buscaron un lugar donde *esconderse*.

La extraña marcha del viejo reloj continuó
con la **8ª** campanada **tocando** aburrida.
Entonces,
uno tras otro,
salieron flotando en fila india
cuatro fantasmas
que lanzaron **aterradores gemidos**
(salían de sus barrigas)
y caminaron derechitos a la cocina
a por un *piscolabis de medianoche*.

La **escalofrian**te campanada número 9
dio paso al **estriden**te repicar de la número 10
y el décimo tañido se abrió al **espeluznan**te número 11.
Cada insistente sonido daba entrada a otro
más horrible que el anterior y, mientras,
una espantosa niña-calabaza
y su espantoso hermano niño-calabaza
se colgaban y se dejaban llevar
por una macabra (pero alegre)... ¡escalera de jardín!

Número doce:

"Número 12,"

Sonó la 12 campanada y un duendecillo malicioso se rio,
bailando y saltando de alegría.
Y **justo** en ese **momento**,
cuando cualquier otro reloj habría parado de sonar,
éste, extraño y excéntrico de estruendo estridente,

no lo hizo.

Al contrario, dio un resonante, enérgico,
y ruidoso tañido número

13!

Después solo se escuchó el *tictac* del reloj en el silencio de la noche...

y... subiendo sin hacer ruido...

andando de puntillas...

hacia la habitación de la niña... al final del pasillo

abren la puerta, *chirríííííían* las bisagras...
¡Es hora de hacer cosas perversas!
Andando en silencio,
andando sin ser vistos,
cuando acaba la cuenta,
¡las monstruosas maldades comienzan a...!

«Uno»

«Dos»

«Tres»

«Cuatro»

«Cinco»

«Seis»

«Siete»

«Ocho»

«Nueve»

«Diez»

«Once»

«Doce»

dijo de repente
una voz inesperada.

«¿¡Trece?!»,

¡chilló un coro horrorizado
de fantasmas asustados!
El viscoso, el arácnido, el alado
y el resto de esperpentos,
se sumieron en el más completo desorden.
«¡Perseguir!,¡acorralar!,¡ atormentar!»,
berreaban.

«¡¡Corred!!».

«¡¡Corred!!».

El **monstruoso alboroto** de la confusión,
dio paso al *silencio* de un cementerio,
cuando el grupo de fantasmas se dio cuenta de que...
el misterioso culpable de esta trama había sido
su *pequeña* **amiga**,
la **bromista** en pijama:
una criatura **encantadora** con ideas traviesas.

E incluso a los espectros despistados la cosa les hizo *gracia*,
porque la niña estaba *muerta de risa*,
demasiado muerta de risa para espantar a *ninguna cosa*.

Y muy entrada la madrugada
jugaron bajo la luz verde de la luna,
mientras el viento soplaba con fuerza
y la vieja casa crujía y crujía.
Era una noche tranquila y normal,
en una casa *algo* especial
en la que habitan
  un fantasma,
     un esperpento,
      un duende,
    un algo,
      o cualquier
          cosa...

y una niña pequeña que tiene un reloj que no cuenta hasta doce
sino hasta un espeluznante... y estremecedor... ¡número *trece!*